BLESSED ARE YOU

THE BEATITUDES OF JESUS IN SCRIPTURE AND IN LIFE

Resource Book

John C. Purdy

the KERYGMA
program

INTRODUCTION

You are walking along a narrow road that climbs steadily upward. You are one of many who go that Way – old and young, male and female, strong and halting. Far ahead, obscured as if by mists and clouds, is your goal. From time to time some of you catch glimpses of it. It is a city of indescribable beauty, where all hungers are appeased and all sorrows end. It is your heart's true home. You name it for one another in different ways: The Kingdom of Heaven, the City of God, the New Jerusalem. In this you are all agreed: It promises a far better future than the present place you occupy.

To encourage one another you sing the praises of the city in familiar hymns: "Lift Every Voice and Sing," "Jerusalem the Golden," "Glorious Things of Thee are Spoken," "Onward, Christian Soldiers."

The journey to God's Kingdom proves longer than you first thought. Nor is this high and narrow Way a detour around life's difficulties. You encounter every kind of suffering known to humans: hunger, thirst, sickness, pain, sorrow, war, temptation, anxiety, depression. Sometimes you quarrel; often you weep; occasionally you despair.

From time to time you come upon side roads. Many of these are broad, inviting boulevards that lead down and away from the Way. There is talk among you of the bliss that might be found at the end of these roads, but the wise among you warn that they will prove to be dead end streets.

You are often tempted to turn back. There is no gate or barrier to prevent you. But when you turn around and look back, you see an empty cross. Its shadow falls across the way you have come. Everything you have experienced is covered by that shadow.

As people do who travel together on long journeys, you tell one another stories. You like to hear about other pilgrims who have gone this Way before. Above all you want to hear about the Hero who blazed this trail. For you are His followers. You are comforted, exhorted, enlightened by signs that He has left for you along the Way. They bear such messages as these:

Blessed are the poor in spirit,
  for theirs is the kingdom of heaven.

Blessed are the merciful,
  for they will receive mercy.

Blessed are those who hunger and thirst for righteousness,
  for they will be filled.

The Way of Discipleship

This metaphor of pilgrims journeying along the Way seems especially useful for a study of the Beatitudes. When I was writing this series I tried out my ideas with the Bible Perspectives Class of the First Presbyterian Church in Santa Fe, New Mexico. For the final session of our study, I fastened to the blackboard a strip of shelf paper with a crude drawing. It showed a group of people traveling a road leading to a better future. Along the way were billboards bearing individual Beatitudes. (It did not occur to me until later to draw the cross at the beginning of the road.) I told the group that this drawing, however crude and child-like, represented the Way of Discipleship. I thought it was a faithful picture of the Christian life as presented in Matthew's Gospel and as reflected in the Beatitudes we had been discussing.

There were other pictures I might have drawn. I might have shown runners on a track; the author of the Book of Hebrews urges us to "run with perseverance the race that is set before us." (12:1) I might have drawn a battle scene; the author of Ephesians counsels us, "Put on the whole armor of God ... for our struggle is not against enemies of blood and flesh, but against the rulers, against the authorities, against ... cosmic powers ... spiritual forces of evil." (6:11-12) I might have shown farmers tending their fields, for James tells us, "The farmer waits for the precious crop ... being patient with it." (5:7)

However, the metaphor of the pilgrim band ascending the highway to the Kingdom of God seems to fit Matthew's Gospel. It corresponds to the well-accepted notion that Matthew was written as a manual of discipleship. It also seems to match our own experience. Many of us are the descendants of immigrants, who came seeking a better country. Some of us are the descendants of slaves who risked everything in a perilous journey to places of freedom. For all of us there is the memory of the People of Promise, liberated from Egypt, making their way through the wilderness, drawn by a vision of a land flowing with milk and honey. See how well that imagery corresponds to these features of the Beatitudes:

- Notice their *futuristic bent*. Each Beatitude is a promise of a better future: "Theirs is the kingdom of heaven ... they will be comforted ... they will inherit the earth."

- Note the *congregational dimension* of the Beatitudes. They are addressed, not to individuals, but to persons going along the Way together. Jesus spoke in plurals, to "those who mourn ... those who hunger and thirst after righteousness ... peacemakers." You cannot be merciful alone, nor can you make peace in a closet.

- The imagery of the Pilgrim Way also preserves the dual meaning of the Beatitudes; they are not only promises of God's favor in the future, but recipes for *happiness right here and now*. "Blessed" signifies happiness; true happiness, which is found in losing oneself in great adventures, in overcoming difficulties, in meeting challenges.

- In addition, by reading the Beatitudes as *signs* along the Way, we are kept from trying to make them into a set of rules. True, Jesus in his Sermon on the Mount is a second Moses, and there are those who read the Beatitudes as the New Commandments. But we know other beatitudes in Scripture: "Blessed are you, Simon son of Jonah! For flesh and blood has not revealed this to you, but my Father in heaven." (Matthew 16:17) "Blessed are those who have not seen and yet have come to believe." (John 20:29) Even if we could force the Beatitudes in Matthew 5:1-12 into a system of rules, we would still have to ask: What does the Lord require of us? And the meaning of the Beatitudes seems most clear when they are treated as signs rather than rules.

The Beatitudes in their Setting

The Beatitudes are part of a larger literary work, the Gospel of Matthew. A Gospel is an account of the life, teachings, death, and resurrection of Jesus. Scholars are generally agreed that the Gospel attributed to Matthew, one of the twelve original disciples, was written late in the first century A.D. Most likely, however, it was not written by the disciple, but by an anonymous teacher who may have used a collection of Jesus' sayings compiled by Matthew as one of his sources.

Matthew is constructed as a brief biography, with five sections of Jesus' teachings interspersed with the narrative. The first of these sections of teachings is the Sermon on the Mount. It consists of chapters five to seven and contains some of Jesus's most familiar words: The Lord's Prayer and such sayings as "Turn the other cheek" and "Go the second mile."

The Beatitudes stand at the beginning of the Sermon on the Mount. If you have never read the Sermon, do so before you begin your study of the Beatitudes. As you read, ask yourself: How shall I think of the Beatitudes in relation to the Sermon? as a preface? as a preamble? as a summary? That is one of the discoveries you will want to make for yourself during this course of study.

The Design of the Study

One of the fruits of this study will be to give you a greater familiarity with Matthew's Gospel. Each session is focused on one or two of the Beatitudes.[1] To provide background for understanding Jesus' words, a narrative from the Old Testament is compared and contrasted with one from the Gospel. You are then encouraged to relate the Beatitudes to individual and congregational life today.

This design was carefully chosen. It sets the Beatitudes in the larger context of Matthew without forcing the reader to make an exhaustive study of the whole before going to each part. Also, it is faithful to the spirit of Matthew.[2] Of the four Gospels, the first seems the most clearly "Jewish." As the introduction to Matthew in the *New Oxford Annotated Bible* says, "Much of the material peculiar to this Gospel is concerned with the Jews or with the fulfillment of Old Testament prophecies." Some scholars conclude that the audience for which the Gospel was originally written was Jewish in background. So it seems faithful to the Gospel author to follow his lead in paying serious attention to the Hebrew Scriptures. It is also faithful to the spirit of Jesus, who is quoted in the Sermon on the Mount as saying this of those Scriptures, "Do not think that I have come to abolish the law or the prophets; I have not come to abolish but to fulfill." (5:17)

An Invitation and a Challenge

Some studies are invitations to journeys; this study is an invitation to interrupt your journey. Take time to read the signs along the Way of Discipleship. Pause and reflect on where you are going and how it is going with your congregation. Above all, sit down and share

---

1 I have slightly modified the order of the sayings in Matthew to group the Beatitudes into six sessions.

2 Several of the Beatitudes have parallels in Luke 6:20-23. For this study, however, we will concentrate on Matthew in order to encourage a broader understanding of that Gospel.

stories. Each of the Beatitudes invites such stories - stories about those who weep, who forgive, who make peace, who are persecuted, who know poverty of spirit. Listen to tales about mourners and peacemakers and persecuted prophets. Hear about Ruth, Naomi, Amos, Esther, Elijah. Learn of Jesus' encounters with Peter, with a pesky Canaanite woman, with an enthusiastic crowd. Listen to the Parable of the Unforgiving Servant. Hear about people of our own time who have been prophets of righteousness, rescuers, peacemakers, comforters.

As your study progresses, keep always in mind the One who has gone before you on the Way. As in all Bible study, seek to hear the compelling voice of Jesus Christ, our Lord and Savior.

Preparing for the First Session

Each person brings different skills and expectations to this study and will develop his or her own method of preparation. At the outset we suggest this approach. Note that each chapter begins with a **Summary**. The **Basic Bible References** for the chapter follow. These passages are the primary ones you should read to prepare for the group session. They are printed in bold type in the text. A **Word List** containing terms or phrases from the Bible references or this *Resource Book* which may be new to you is also included. Some of these may be explained in the notes of your Bible. For additional background you may eventually want to look them up in a Bible dictionary.

Now, read the summary and skim the chapter, without looking up Bible references, to gain an overview of the material. Next go back and carefully read the chapter, reviewing the Bible references. Use the margins or a separate sheet of paper to make comments or note questions you want to discuss.

At the end of each chapter you will find several items **For Further Study and Reflection**. The first section recommends texts to be included in your "Memory Bank." These are familiar passages that are so central to knowledge of the Bible that you should be able to recall their content or to recite them. The second section suggests "Research" projects which will enrich your grasp of the material, but are not essential. Lastly, there are comments and questions for "Reflection" which will challenge you to explore further the issues raised in the chapter.

Introducing John C. Purdy

Mr. Purdy is a graduate of the College of Wooster (B.A.) and Princeton Theological Seminary (M.Div.); he also spent a year of study in Basel, Switzerland. Following Seminary,

Mr. Purdy was a pastor in Wisconsin for 12 years. For the 26 years prior to his retirement, he was Curriculum Editor for the Presbyterian Church (U.S.A.).

He is the author of the popular Kerygma study, *Lord, Teach Us to Pray: Six Studies on Spirituality and the Lord's Prayer*. He has also written *Parables at Work* (Westminster Press, 1985) and *Returning God's Call: The Challenge of Christian Living* (Westminster Press, 1989) and edited the volume *Always Being Reformed: The Future of Church Education* (Geneva Press, 1985). For five years, Mr. Purdy wrote the monthly "Questions and Answer" column for the magazine *Presbyterian Survey*.

SUMMARY

Poverty may be either a spiritual or a material condition – or both at once. Neither kind of poverty is necessarily a hindrance to happiness. Jesus promised blessedness even to those who were bankrupt.

BASIC BIBLE REFERENCES

1 Kings 17:8-24
Matthew 5:3; 19:16-22

WORD LIST

blessed
eternal life
happiness
kingdom of heaven
poor in spirit
poverty
treasure
wealth

1

THE POOR IN SPIRIT

Blessed are the poor in spirit,
for theirs is the kingdom of heaven.
(MATTHEW 5:3)

A Happy Man

The Valentine's Day issue of the *New Yorker* profiled a happy man. He was living in a comfortable home in Vermont. One of his four sons was a student at Harvard, another a Harvard graduate. The third was studying music at Curtis Institute in Philadelphia. The fourth lived in New York City, where he restored and sold vintage motorcycles. Their father had enough private income that he could spend every day at what he liked best, writing historical novels. His writing had produced so much money that he established his own welfare fund, administered by his wife. The man in the *New Yorker* profile was the Russian author, Aleksandr Solzhenitsyn.

If he felt especially blessed, it was because he had also known the most extreme privation. His autobiographical novel, *One Day in the Life of Ivan Denisovich*, tells about a bitter cold January day in a forced labor camp. Ivan (Solzhenitsyn's alter ego) sits down to a supper of bread with watery soup:

> He began to eat. He started with the watery stuff on the top and drank it right down. The warmth went through his body and his insides were sort of quivering waiting for that gruel to come down. It was great! This was what a prisoner lived for, this one little moment.[1]

A Widow in Canaan

Only those who have been desperate for daily bread know the full meaning of poverty – and the blessedness of having a sufficiency. Aleksandr Solzhenitsyn has a soul mate in the

---

1 Aleksandr Solzhenitsyn, *One Day in the Life of Ivan Denisovich* (New York: Frederick A . Praeger, Inc., 1963), p. 169.

Widow of Zarephath, whose story is told in **1 Kings 17:8-24**. Scan the background of the story in 17:1-7; then carefully read the rest of the chapter.

When we first meet this woman, she has three strikes against her. She is a Canaanite; her people are among those Israel wished to drive from the country. She is a widow in a society where a husband was considered essential as provider and protector. But worst of all, her land is suffering a terrible drought. She has only a few scraps of food for herself and her child. She is gathering sticks for a last fire; she and her son will eat what they have and prepare to die.

Along comes Elijah, the mighty prophet of Israel, and everything is changed. The woman's three strikes become three blessings. God has chosen the widow to take the prophet into her home. With this special man in her house, the widow is guaranteed protection. And her few bits of food are miraculously multiplied to outlast the drought and famine!

But happiness, as it sometimes does, proves fickle. The widow's son sickens and dies. And, with the death of her son, she lost her social security. The child was her one hope for the future. Woe upon woe! To her grief and anxiety is added the cruel burden of guilt. "What have you against me, O man of God?" she cries out to Elijah. "You have come to bring my sin to remembrance, and to cause the death of my son." (17:18) Such self-loathing indicates a poverty of spirit worse than any emptiness of cupboard or purse.

Enter happiness again, this time in a new and wonderful form. In answer to the prayers of Elijah, God restores the child to life. The joy of the widow must be as great as that of Mary in the resurrection account in John; she was weeping for her dead Master when he encountered her in the garden. Hope restored must be doubly sweet.

The story in 1 Kings ends with the widow's profession: "Now I know that you are a man of God, and that the word of the Lord in your mouth is truth." (17:24) To hope and love is added faith.

A Rich Young Man in Judea

Now read the story of Jesus and the Rich Young Man, which Matthew tells in **19:16-22**. The details are familiar: The man accosts Jesus, asking for the secret of eternal life. As you will see in verse 20, Jesus draws out the admission that the young man has kept all God's commandments, but still feels something is missing. Jesus tells him: "Sell your possessions and give the money to the poor, and you will have treasure in heaven." Then Jesus invites him to become a disciple. "When the young man heard this word, he went away grieving, for he had many possessions." (19:22)

Stories of the unhappy rich are not unfamiliar to us. A generation of young people was shocked, when in April 1994 the rock star Kurt Cobain put a shotgun to his head and pulled the trigger. He was the lead signer of Nirvana, a musical group wildly popular with youth. Cobain had fame, money, a wife, a child – everything, seemingly, to live for. But evidently at the core of his life was emptiness; something vital was missing.

Comparing the Widow and the Rich Young Man

The biblical accounts of the Widow of Zarephath and the Rich Young Man have similarities. Details in Kings suggest that the woman may have been well off. Mention is made of "her household"; possibly she had servants. Both the widow and the young man encounter charismatic men of God. Through the agency of Elijah, the woman experiences great happiness, the restoration of a lost child. To the young man is offered the ultimate in happiness: Jesus tells him that if he sells everything and gives to the poor, he will have treasure in heaven; he will have a huge bank balance of blessedness with God. What else can "treasure in heaven" mean? Those who have "treasure in heaven" have investments in the Better Future.

The present generation of older adults in my nation knows the opposite of having investments in the future. We have mortgaged the future with enormous debts and deficits. As one study of the United States says, "From the early 1970's forward … America instituted a fundamental shift in its allocation of resources: from the future to the present, from investment to consumption, from young to old."[2]

Many affluent older people have put their entitlements ahead of the welfare of their grandchildren. Mortgaging the future is what "treasure in heaven" most definitely does *not* mean; in fact, it means quite the opposite.

Yet most of us cannot entertain the idea of surrendering financial security. Nor could the Rich Young Man open his hands to receive such a great blessing. He could not let go of his wealth. And so he went away sorrowful. He asked Jesus the price of happiness; it proved too high. He was a wiser but infinitely sadder human being.

Consider the two main characters in our stories: The widow was able to receive what was given. She in her grief and despair was made rich. But the young man with great material riches was left impoverished in spirit.

---

2 William Strauss and Neil Howe, *Generations: The History of America's Future, 1584 to 2069* (New York: William Morrow and Company, Inc., 1991), p. 387.

We can identify with both the widow and the young man. Like her, we often need God's sustenance, comfort, healing, forgiveness, word of promise. In the Lord's Prayer we ask for bread, for forgiveness, for help against evil. And, like the young man, we sometimes have more than we need, while others are impoverished. In this case, our abundance is a hindrance to discipleship. So in the Lord's Prayer we plead for the coming of God's Kingdom on earth. Surely that includes the end of famine, injustice, poverty, and despair.

Signs Along the Way

"Blessed are the poor in spirit," said Jesus, "for theirs is the kingdom of heaven." If we imagine ourselves as pilgrims along the way, what might be the meaning of this saying?

Sometimes we find ourselves walking in the shoes of the Widow of Zarephath. So overcome are we with despair that we think we must have wandered down a wrong path. We ask of anyone who will listen: Why did God let my child die? Why is there not enough money to keep body and soul together? Why does famine fall upon innocent women and children? Why wouldn't it be better just to lie down and die?

To such conditions the first Beatitude is a promise: Happiness is also for us who now are poor in spirit. We dare not turn back. We should not stop walking. We can't give in to the temptation to lie down and go to sleep. Our feelings of desperation are symptoms of need; they are not burdens laid on us by Blind Necessity. God's Kingdom, God's presence and rule, are promised to us.

Sometimes it is not despair that slows or stops us on the Way. It is the weight of wealth. Abundance tempts us to think that we have arrived. Surely this is heaven, this wealth of houses and lands and goods and clothing and food and entertainment. Then the Beatitude becomes an admonition: material blessings, which are sustenance for the journey, have gotten confused with final rewards. Material comfort as an end in itself is a dead end. We had better consider lightening the load!

In Every Congregation

At any given moment, there are Christians in every congregation who represent those two conditions. There are those who suffer a desperate poverty of spirit. They are crushed by their failures, they are stymied by the circumstances which surround them. Who of us cannot think of at least one member of our church who enjoys no blessedness at all, who despairs of ever being happy?

A poignant example comes to mind from my five years of writing a Question and Answer column for a denominational magazine. The pointed inquiry began:

> I am a chronically, severely mentally disabled person church members seem to all but shun. It hurts me. Why?

The letter writer went on to explain that she had been diagnosed as schizophrenic, but with the help of medication was able to function reasonably well. Surely in many congregations there are folks like her, who are not easy to have around, but whose spirits are being crushed by indifference or worse, avoidance.

And in every congregation there are some who are considerably better off than the rest. Not every church has a Rich Young Man. But in nearly each congregation there are a few who have more than enough and to spare. Just as a few desperately unhappy people can drain the energy out of a church, so can envy of another's wealth. Some people make themselves miserable by continually measuring their income against the incomes of those more fortunate. Envy is no more a happy state than discouragement, dependency or even schizophrenia.

Jesus' Beatitude speaks to both situations – to congregations where there are desperately unhappy folk and to those where there is crippling envy of wealth. It encourages those who are happy and well-adjusted not to give up on the emotionally needy. It also warns both rich and poor that God's blessing cancels out the disparities of wealth. All may be counted among the followers of Jesus; none are excluded.

But surely the Beatitude is also an invitation, a summons to seek more out of life, to "reach for the brass ring," to make more out of each day, to pursue happiness with greater hope and zeal. Neither poverty of purse nor poverty of spirit are necessarily permanent conditions.

There is a shining moment in the life of the hero in George Bernanos' *The Diary of a Country Priest*. The young man, afflicted with a malignancy, is trudging along the road when he is offered his first ride on a motorcycle. He confesses to the reader:

> I was never young because I never dared be young. Around me, no doubt, life went on and my companions knew and tasted that wondrous bitter spring, whilst I tried not to think of it and drugged myself with work. Many of them were very fond of me, no doubt. But the best of my friends must have shrunk in spite of

themselves from the mark my earliest childhood had left on me: a little boy's knowledge of poverty and the shame of it.

Then comes the fellow with the motorbike.

And by a presentiment which I cannot explain, I also understood, I *knew* that God did not wish me to die without knowing something of that risk — just enough, maybe, for my sacrifice to be complete when the time came. For one poor short moment I was to taste that glory.[3]

To any who have for whatever reason never risked happiness, Jesus' Beatitude is an offer of a glorious ride. To those, who like the rich young man, are "stuck" with their wealth. To those who have let the pinch of poverty spoil their lives. To those who never dared to be young at heart. To each the Beatitude says: Go for it! Take the risk, take the trip, seize the moment, *now*.

FOR FURTHER STUDY AND REFLECTION

Memory Bank

Matthew 5:3

Research

1. Read through ten or a dozen psalms, looking for expressions of both material and spiritual poverty. Include Psalm 88, which might have been composed by someone with a lifelong illness. How do these expressions compare with your understanding of what it means to be "poor in spirit"?

2. In the NRSV the Greek word *makarios* is translated "Blessed." Look at several other versions of the Bible to see how the word is rendered in English. Note also how the rest of Matthew 5:3 reads. Which translation do you prefer? Why?

Reflection

1. Meditate on the following comments which Dietrich Bonhoeffer wrote to a friend from a prison cell:

---

3 George Bernanos, *The Diary of a Country Priest* (New York: The Macmillan Company, 1937), p. 184.

So you think the Bible has very little to say about health, fortune, vigour, etc. That is certainly not true of the Old Testament. The intermediate theological category between God and human fortune is, it seems to me, that of blessing. There is indeed no concern for fortune in the Old Testament, but there is a concern for the blessing of God, which includes all earthly blessings as well.[4]

... I am sure we ought to love God in our *lives* and in all the blessings he sends us. We should trust him in our lives, so that when our time comes, but not before, we may go to him in love and trust and joy. But, speaking frankly, to long for the transcendent when you are in your wife's arms is, to put it mildly, a lack of taste, and it is certainly not what God expects of us. We ought to find God and love him in the blessings he sends us. If he pleases to grant us some overwhelming earthly bliss, we ought not to try and be more religious than God himself.[5]

2. Write a brief prayer, in which you expand "Give us this day our daily bread" into requests for whatever else you need to make you truly happy.

3. The governments of some nations assign to humans God-given rights that include life, liberty and the pursuit of happiness. How do you understand the relationship of such human rights to Jesus' statement, "Blessed are the poor in spirit"?

---

4 Dietrich Bonhoeffer, *Letters and Papers from Prison* (New York: The Macmillan Company, 1953), p .231.
5 Ibid., p. 113.

Blessed Are You

SUMMARY

Many are bitter because of their social situation, which enforces a submission they both resent and resist. Even such bitterness stands under Jesus' promise of happiness; it can be transformed into rejoicing.

BASIC BIBLE REFERENCES

The Book of Ruth
Matthew 5:4, 5; 15:21-28

WORD LIST

Canaanite
gleaning
inheritance
meek
meekness
Moabite

2

THE MOURNERS AND
THE MEEK

Blessed are those who mourn, for they will be comforted.
Blessed are the meek, for they will inherit the earth.
(MATTHEW 5:4, 5)

A Story from Dachau

Dr. Carol Smith, a retired pediatrician, was a member of the study group in Sante Fe with whom I tested this material. One Sunday morning we had time for a private visit. She told me about her husband, Marcus. As a young army physician he was sent in the spring of 1945 to the infamous labor camp of Dachau. It was not until decades later that he was able to write about the misery of the place. In his book, *The Harrowing of Hell*, he describes how his team of specialists helped over 30,000 foreign laborers prepare to return to their homelands.

If any group of people fit all descriptions of "those who mourn," and "the meek," it is those described in Smith's book. Although the war in Europe had ended, they were not released at once. Immediate repatriation was impossible. Most were physically unfit to travel; transportation was unavailable. For several months they were kept under guard, regimented, documented – with no choice but to submit. Most of them had memories of torture, abuse, and privation. Some had seen loved ones killed. Many had no contact with their families for five years.

The Story of Ruth

For this session we have combined the second and third Beatitudes. It seems that the theme which links these two sayings is "Crying for a Helper," weeping in despair and pleading for someone to help. Those who thus mourn and are meek are promised comfort and inheritance. As scriptural background for the chapter we will begin with Ruth. While the context of that book differs from the situation of the prisoners at Dachau, there are some similarities. The pivotal character in Ruth is a widow, a refugee, a displaced person. Sorrow, meekness, and inheritance are major themes of her story.

Turn now to the book of **Ruth**. It has only four chapters, and you will be able to grasp the story line quickly. Note especially Ruth's background. She was not a Jew; she was a Moabite. Her in-laws, Elimelech and Naomi, had fled to Moab from famine in their native Bethlehem. Elimelech died. So did Ruth's husband, leaving her childless. Naomi got word that things were better in Bethlehem and determined to go back home. She advised Ruth to stay in her own country, but Ruth in a devoted kind of meekness said to her mother-in-law:

> Do not press me to leave you or turn back from following you! Where you go, I will go; where you lodge, I will lodge; your people shall be my people; and your God my God. (1:16)

When the women arrived in Bethlehem, Naomi took no comfort in being home again:

> Call me no longer Naomi (which means Pleasant), call me Mara (which means Bitter), for the Almighty has dealt bitterly with me. (1:20)

Naomi had cause to be bitter. There was a plot of land that belonged to Elimelech, but as a woman she could not claim it. In Israel's patriarchal culture, women had no inheritance. So the two widows got on as best they could, with Ruth going into the fields to glean. She went where the grain was being reaped; she followed the harvesters, meekly picking up scraps. Her gleanings were what the women had to eat.

The field where Ruth gleaned was owned by Boaz, who happened to be a distant relative of Elimelech. Boaz was impressed by Ruth's modesty and meekness. He told his workers not to molest her, and he gave her extra grain to take home. Naomi quickly saw a way to provide for her daughter-in-law. She told Ruth to go at night to the threshing floor and to lie down at the feet of Boaz. Risking her reputation, perhaps her life, Ruth did as she was told. And Boaz, a gentle man, did not take advantage of Ruth when he awoke. On the contrary, he resolved to marry her.

According to the customs of that day, if Boaz should marry Ruth, he would acquire along with her the right to buy the land that had belonged to Elimelech. But there was a hitch. There was a relative closer to Elimelech than Boaz. However, when that relative saw that he would have to take Ruth along with the land, and thus damage his own inheritance, he forswore any rights. And so Boaz married Ruth and exercised his right to buy the land. Naomi and Ruth were fully integrated into the economy. In time, Ruth bore Boaz a son – whom Naomi claimed also. And this son, Obed, was the grandfather of King David and one of the forebears of Jesus of Nazareth. And so, in Shakespeare's words: "All losses are restored, and sorrows end."

The Canaanite Woman

For a companion story to Ruth, read **Matthew 15:21-28**. There Jesus encounters a Canaanite woman. When he first meets her she seems anything but meek. He had gone away from Galilee into the neighboring territory of Tyre and Sidon, probably to rest. The woman, a Gentile from that region, came to him and pleaded with him to heal her daughter. The child was demon-possessed.

Jesus tried to put off the anguished mother. He told her that he was sent to the Jews, not to Gentiles. But she would not desist. She got down on her knees and begged for help. Jesus said bluntly, "It is not fair to take the children's food and throw it to the dogs." (15:26) With a terrible meekness she replied, "Yes, Lord, yet even the dogs eat the crumbs that fall from their masters' table." (15:27) In turn, Jesus showed the meekness of those who are willing to be taught. He answered her, "Woman, great is your faith! Let it be done for you as you wish." (15:28) And it was done. The child was healed.

I have been amazed at how that story resonates with contemporary folk. I once used it as the Bible study for a weekend retreat. When we had our closing worship, members of the congregation were invited to respond publicly and spontaneously to the narrative. A preacher from Puerto Rico praised the courage of the Canaanite woman. In his country, he said, any woman who accosted a man like that in public would be called a prostitute. A divorced woman who had been left to bring up a daughter said with deep emotion, "That's my story." And a college student wept as she identified herself with the daughter; she had been addicted to drugs before faith in Christ set her free.

About Comfort and Inheritance

Surely it is not hard for us to empathize with Ruth, Naomi, and the Canaanite woman. They knew what it was like to be powerless, to live on the margins of their culture. They experienced the bitter tears of despair and cried out for help. Correspondingly, they all received great comfort. But like many women in many cultures, the only way they could get what they needed was through submission. This kind of meekness was their only option.

But what about inheritance? "Blessed are the meek," said Jesus, "for they will inherit the earth." In the story of Ruth we saw how desperately important was the inheritance of the land. If you were cut off from the land, you were cut off from a decent livelihood. You became a marginal person. To "inherit the earth" was no metaphor for Naomi and Ruth. Unless their family owned land, they were dependent on the charity of others.

The story of the Canaanite woman raises the question of inheritance in a different way. She was, as Jesus rightly perceived, a Gentile who stood outside of the inheritance promised to Israel. When he said to her that it was not right to take the children's bread and throw it to the dogs, he was probably being ironic. Still, the message was plain enough: his mission was to Israel.

In the tradition of the Christian Church, both the Book of Ruth and Matthew 15:21-28 have been understood as missionary stories. Neither Ruth nor the Canaanite woman were born into Israel, and yet the promises of God were extended to include them. These stories tell us that faithfulness, not race or gender, is what finally matters. It is faith alone that assures acceptance into the people of promise; the future belongs to the faithful. Blood, race, inheritance, parentage, gender, social status, ethnic identity do not assure us a place at Jesus' table. Faith in Christ alone gives access.

It is necessary for congregations to be reminded of that. We tend to shut our doors against folks who are not of "our kind." People who look different, talk with an accent, or were born in other cultures are not always given full acceptance.

In doing so, we rob ourselves. Even those who seem to offer us nothing but their suffering and misery can be a blessing. For example, some congregations have had wonderful experiences in sponsoring war refugees. Following World War II, the congregation in Chicago where my father-in-law was pastor sponsored a Yugoslavian/German couple. Following the war in southeast Asia, the congregation in Pennsylvania where my mother was an elder sponsored a family from Viet Nam. I am happy to report that both families got along very well and enriched the lives of those congregations.

Not only war refugees know, like Ruth, what it means to labor in fields belonging to others. In Ralph Ellison's novel *Invisible Man*, the narrator tells us about his grandfather, who had been born in slavery:

> On his deathbed he called my father to him and said, "Son, after I'm gone I want you to keep up the good fight. I never told you, but our life is a war and I have been a traitor all my born days, a spy in the enemy's country ever since I give up my gun back in the Reconstruction. Live with your head in the lion's mouth. I want you to overcome 'em with yeses, undermine 'em with grins, agree 'em to death and destruction, let 'em swoller you till they vomit or bust wide

open." They thought the old man had gone out of his mind. He had been the meekest of men ... "Learn it to the younguns," he whispered fiercely; then he died.[1]

There are all sorts of persons living among us who have had to use meekness as a strategy to make a place for themselves. Climb your family tree and you will probably find immigrants, slaves, indentured servants, refugees, displaced persons, prisoners of war, poor widows and orphans.

The Infirm Elderly

My dictionary has several definitions of meekness: "enduring injury with patience and without resentment"; "deficient in spirit and courage"; "not violent or strong." Those phrases bring to mind the elderly in the private nursing home I visited as a young pastor. Many were sunk so deep in grief and dependency that they were almost inert. Their sadness was so palpable that I'd come home from an afternoon at the nursing home with a splitting headache.

Doesn't your congregation include some of these infirm or invalid elderly? Are not some of them refugees? Is not their hearts' home a time and place somewhere in the past? A time and place to which there is no hope of return? The present, with its changes in values and technology, seems to many of the elderly like a foreign land. Theirs is an enforced meekness. They have no choice but to be submissive, even though their custodians mean them well and provide food and medicine and blankets.

How can we show to the infirm elderly that we share an inheritance? How can we show them that they have their place among us, that they belong to us and with us in every important way?

FOR FURTHER STUDY AND REFLECTION

Memory Bank

> Ruth 1:16
> Matthew 5:4, 5

---

1 Ralph Ellison, *Invisible Man* (New York: Signet Books, 1947), pp. 19-20.

Research

1. If you have a Bible in a language other than English, see how Matthew 5:4-5 is rendered. Make your own translation and compare it with several English versions.

2. Go through the Book of Ruth and underscore the words "bless," "blessed" and "blessing." Note the contexts in which these words occur. Who blesses whom? What does the blessing involve?

3. Make a list of words or phrases you associate with meekness. To what extent is submission central to your description? What other qualities are included? How do you relate these qualities to the stories in this chapter?

4. Psalm 137 is a lamentation of Israel during the exile in Babylon. Consider how difficult it must have been to "sing the LORD's song in a foreign land." Look for other psalms of lamentation. Are those who mourn promised comfort in these psalms? In what ways?

Reflection

1. Writing in the *Christian Century*, Walter Wink says:

   > Increasingly women, peasants, gays, minorities, people of color and laborers are becoming aware of the systemic nature of the Powers arrayed against them. Many have tried to oppose their exploiters by means of the very violence used to keep them in check, only to discover that violence, once employed, is not easily renounced … How can evil be vanquished without our creating new evils and becoming evil ourselves?[2]

   Think about this question in relationship to your understanding of Matthew 5:4-5.

2. In this session the second and third Beatitudes were considered together. What advantages did you find in looking at these sayings at the same time? In what ways do mourning and meekness often go together?

3. In the Book of Ruth an underlying assumption is that marriage and sons are primary sources of a woman's security and value. What is your evaluation of this assumption? What would you suggest as sources for esteem and happiness for contemporary women? How are these related to your understanding of the Beatitude on meekness?

---

2   Walter Wink, "The Other World Is Here," *The Christian Century* (April 27, 1994), p. 443.

SUMMARY

Mercy begets mercy; forgiveness begets forgiveness. Because God's mercy is steadfast and everlasting, there are no limits on our forgiveness of one another. Forgiveness brings peace and blessedness.

BASIC BIBLE REFERENCES

Genesis 32:3-33:11
Matthew 5:7; 18:21-35

WORD LIST

birthright
forgiveness
mercy

3

THE MERCIFUL

Blessed are the merciful,
for they will receive mercy.
(MATTHEW 5:7)

In a Town "Cleansed" of Moslems, Serb Church Will Crown the Deed, read the headline. 40,000 Muslim inhabitants had been driven out, the newspaper reported. The Serb mayor took the reporter to the top of a ridge overlooking the city. He showed him a wooden cross he had erected. Then the mayor said, "The Turks destroyed the Serbian church that was here when they arrived in Zvornik in 1463. Now we are rebuilding the church and reclaiming this as Serbian land forever and ever."

Violence begets violence; the cycle of injury and vengeance, injury and vengeance, seems to go on forever. "Getting even" is almost as old as time. One of the first phrases we learned as children was, "I'll get even with you if it's the last thing I do." We said this not only to the neighborhood bully or the kids from the other side of town; we said it to sisters and brothers.

Esau and Jacob

If ever there was a brother who wanted to get even, it was Esau, the twin of Jacob. Their story is one of the first we heard in Sunday School. It is told in Genesis, chapters 25-33. Skim those chapters, beginning at 25:19, or read the subheadings in your Bible to review the main events in the story.

Esau was born first, so all the rights of the first born son came to him – leadership of the clan and a double share of the inheritance. Also, Esau could expect to receive his father's death-bed blessing, which would bestow special gifts. But Jacob, the cleverer of the twins, tricked Esau out of the birthright and out of the blessing, then wisely fled the country. He showed even greater wisdom in staying away for fourteen years.

In **Genesis 32:3-33:11** we have the remarkable story of the reunion of the brothers. Read that material now. Here Jacob is on his way back to the land of his forbearers. He is bringing wives and children and flocks and herds in considerable number. He is rightly terrified of meeting his brother, from whom he can expect nothing but revenge. When it is reported that Esau and his men are approaching, Jacob goes ahead of his wives and children to meet Esau, "bowing himself to the ground seven times, until he came near his brother. But Esau ran to meet him, and embraced him, and fell on his neck and kissed him, and they wept." (33:3, 4)

The story of the reconciliation then moves quickly to a climax in this unexpected request from Jacob, "… if I find favor with you, then accept this present from my hand; for to see your face is like seeing the face of God – since you have received me with such favor." (33:10)

At stake in this reunion was the future of the people of Israel. Jacob's sons were to become the heads of the twelve tribes. Esau's mercy was a hinge on which the continuation of the people turned. Had Esau indulged in a bit of "ethnic cleansing," what would have become of the Israelites? But once again, the future of Israel was kept open by an act of mercy.

Not a New Commandment

When Jesus said, "Blessed are the merciful," he was not giving out a new commandment. Among the Hebrews, mercy was a cardinal virtue. Mercy was also the single, most important attribute of their Lord. Their songs and prayers abound with praise to God for steadfast love and mercy:

> Surely goodness and mercy shall follow me
> all the days of my life.   (Psalm 23:6)

> The Lord is merciful and gracious,
> slow to anger and abounding in steadfast love.   (Psalm 103:8)

Yet in the third Beatitude it seems that mercy has a severe condition attached to it: "Blessed are the merciful, *for they will receive mercy*." (italics added) Is it possible that only those who themselves forgive can be forgiven? It is not only in this one verse that the notion appears. In the Lord's Prayer we are taught to pray, "And forgive us our debts, as we also have forgiven our debtors." And to that prayer is appended this warning, "For if you forgive others their trespasses, your heavenly Father will also forgive you; but if you do not forgive others, neither will your Father forgive your trespasses." (Matthew 6:12, 14-15)

These passages clearly raise the question of how our willingness to forgive is linked to our receipt of forgiveness.

Does God Keep Score?

Does God keep score? Is there, somewhere in the heavenly places, an account book? Under each of our names is there a list of debits and credits, where each act of forgiveness is set down opposite some mean or nasty thing we have done? No, such is *not* the case, as is clearly shown in one of Jesus' most striking parables. Read the story now in **Matthew 18:21-35**.

According to the Gospel account, Peter came to Jesus and asked about the limits of forgiveness. "Lord, if another member of the church sins against me, how often should I forgive? As many as seven times?" Seven was regarded as a perfect number by Hebrews. One supposes that Peter thought he was being perfectly correct in offering to forgive an offending person seven times.

If you pause between Peter's question and Jesus' answer, you can almost hear a great door turning on its hinge. This is one of those critical moments in the history of ethics. Is there a limit on mercy? Is there a point at which even God says, "Enough, already"?

Jesus said to Peter, "Not seven times, but, I tell you seventy-seven times." (Some Greek manuscripts read "seventy times seven," which suggests an infinite number.) But whether seventy-seven or seventy times seven, Jesus' response indicates that forgiveness is beyond measurement. There is no limit on forgiveness; forgiveness has nothing to do with bookkeeping; mercy does not keep score.

To drive home this point, Jesus told a fantastic story. We know it as The Parable of the Unforgiving Slave. It is important to understand that the parable is a fictional narrative, not a sober account of how the business affairs of humans are carried on. For Jesus told of a slave who was forgiven a debt of millions, but could then not bring himself to forgive a fellow slave a debt of a few dollars.

Once when I was using this parable in a Bible study group, we fell into the trap of treating it as a realistic account. We were discussing the behavior of the unforgiving slave: he went out from the presence of his king, who had just remitted an enormous debt and cancelled an order of imprisonment. Chancing on a fellow slave who owed him a paltry sum and could not pay, he had that poor wretch thrown into prison. One of the members of our group shrugged and said, "Well, that's human nature for you. That's why we talk about total depravity."

But surely Jesus wanted Peter to see the unforgiving slave as a monster! There is no way, psychologically, to account for his behavior. How can one who has himself just been released from a terrible punishment do such a horrible thing to a fellow creature? Where in all of history or literature is there a human beast like the unforgiving slave?

Our group discussed the dynamics of forgiveness. We agreed that we show to others the mercy that is shown to us. If kids are raised "by the book," by parents and teachers who keep a strict accounting and never forgive the slightest mistake, they will themselves be unforgiving. Those who are beaten for giving offense will in turn beat others. But those who are raised in an atmosphere of acceptance will themselves be accepting.

For those who never learn to forgive, the consequences are dire. So says the verse appended to The Parable of the Unforgiving Slave. After we learn that the merciless slave is handed over to be tortured (to force him to reveal any hidden assets), we hear: "So my heavenly Father will also do to every one of you, if you do not forgive your brother or sister from your heart." (18:35)

Hard Hearts Destroy a Family

The truth of that verse is elaborated in the Pulitzer Prize novel by Jane Smiley, *A Thousand Acres*. It is the story of the unhappiness visited on one family whose members could not learn to forgive. The central characters are Laurence Cook, a prosperous Iowa farmer, and his three daughters – Ginny, Rose, and Caroline.

The story begins with the father's decision to retire and to give his rich farm to the three girls. When Caroline, the youngest, demurs, Laurence harshly cuts her out of the deal. But after turning the farm and its operation over to Ginny and Rose and their husbands, the father changes his mind. He wants the property back. A bitter legal battle ensues; Ginny and Rose on one side, Laurence and Caroline on the other.

The family quarrel is not simply over land. Rose forces Ginny to remember what she had for years denied: their father had sexually abused both girls when they were in their teens. The reader wonders how much of the father's anger is hatred of himself turned outward against his daughters.

Meanwhile, Jess Clark has returned to the community after years in the northwestern states. Both Ginny and Rose fall in love with him. When Rose wins him, Ginny determines to poison her. But Rose dies of cancer before her sister can do her in. On her deathbed Rose speaks the words that are key to the family's fortunes:

So all I have is the knowledge that I saw! That I saw without having been afraid and without turning away, and that I didn't forgive the unforgivable. Forgiveness is a reflex for when you can't stand what you know. I resisted that reflex. That's my sole, solitary, lonely accomplishment.[1]

The Cook family is shattered by their resistance to forgiveness. At the novel's end, Rose's husband is also dead – of suicide. Ginny and her husband are estranged; she is working in a Perkins Pancake House. The thousand acre farm has been sold for debts; Ginny and Caroline are saddled with unpaid taxes.

Congregations at Risk

Where forgiveness is resisted, not only families are at risk: Christian congregations will likewise be destroyed if members cannot learn to forgive one another. Disagreements don't destroy churches; the inability or unwillingness of members to forgive one another ruins churches.

How many church fights have you experienced? If you have never belonged to a congregation that has had a major conflict, you are an exception. Building programs are often occasions for battles. I left my first parish because of a deep division over a proposal to build a new church. I have known other congregations to split into factions over money, the pastor, doctrine, even the American flag.

Congregations inevitably have strong disagreements, sometimes ugly brawls. In their book *Generations*, William Strauss and Neil Howe pinpoint one contributing cause: at any given moment in American society, there coexist members of four or five generations. Each generation is as different from the others as cheese is from chalk. Look at the clashes in values among the generation that fought World War II, their children who came to adulthood in the 50s, and the leaders of the "counter culture" in the 60s.

Of course there will be struggles within denominations and their congregations over such matters as ordination, life styles, and inclusive language. Congregations are like families in this respect; there is a constant tug-of-war between the generations. However, it will not be these struggles that do in denominations or congregations, but the inability of members on all sides to forgive one another.

No one ever said forgiveness is easy. But surely the point of Jesus' Parable of the Unforgiving Slave is this: seeing how great is God's mercy toward us, we can be merciful

---

1   Jane Smiley, *A Thousand Acres* (New York: Alfred A. Knopf, 1992), pp. 355-356.

to others. We can forgive because we have been forgiven. And we can find blessedness in the forgiving. Every act of forgiveness is also an act of remembrance; we remember how merciful God has been to us.

Showing Mercy

Who can we look to today an an exemplar? It is difficult – probably impossible – to find one. For as Jesus taught forgiveness it is not an heroic deed. Showing mercy to one another is a small thing when compared to the great mercy God has shown to us. Forgiveness happens all the time. It is what makes marriages and friendships happy. It happens between husbands and wives, among brothers and sisters, friends, fellow church members. It keeps these relationships sweet.

In a parish I served, there were two men on the official board who were always at swords' points. We could not have a meeting without hard words between them. As a young minister I felt that this was my fault – and not only my fault, but a major fault. If church members did not get along, I was not doing my job. With the perspective of age, I now understand two things: severe disagreements are part of congregational life, just as they are of family life. And it is the business of Christians to forgive one another.

The story of the slave who could not forgive a small debt shows an extraordinary violation of the ordinary dynamics of human relations. It is when extraordinary things happen that the Fourth Beatitude comes into play. When the day-by-day aggravations between husband and wife become building blocks of a house of estrangement, both need to hear "Blessed are the merciful, for they will receive mercy." When disagreements over finances or rituals or doctrines in a congregation escalate to a split, then partisans on both sides need to hear, "Blessed are the merciful, for they will receive mercy."

FOR FURTHER STUDY AND REFLECTION

Memory Bank

> Genesis 33:10
> Matthew 5:7

Research

1. Explore the Old Testament notion of "blessing" as it appears in Genesis 25-33, using commentaries and a Bible dictionary.

2. Look in the index of your hymnal for hymns on mercy. Review them to see whether they make the connection between God's mercy and ours.

Reflection

1. Several other stories in the Old Testament provide examples of mercy in action. One which has similarities to the saga of Jacob and Esau is that of Cain and Abel in Genesis 4. Review that chapter to see what is said about mercy.

2. A companion novel to *A Thousand Acres* is Anne Tyler's *Saint Maybe*. Ian Bedloe wanders into the Church of the Second Chance and prays for forgiveness for his role in the death of his brother. He is shocked to discover that asking is not enough. He says to the minister,

   "I thought God forgives everything."

   "He does," Reverend Emmett said, "But you can't just say, 'I'm sorry, God.' Why, anyone could do that much! You have to offer reparation – concrete, practical reparation, according to the rules of our church."[2]

   Reflect on how these remarks are related to, "Blessed are the merciful, for they will receive mercy."

---

2 Anne Tyler, *Saint Maybe* (New York: Alfred A. Knopf, 1991), p. 122.

BLESSED ARE YOU

SUMMARY

The holiness of God requires a corresponding purity on our part. However, purity need not be an obsessive, crippling demand.

BASIC BIBLE REFERENCES

Isaiah 6:1-8
Matthew 5:8; 17:1-8

WORD LIST

glory
holy, holiness
Pharisee
Puritan
purity
sacraments
transfiguration

4

THE PURE IN HEART

Blessed are the pure in heart, for they will see God.
(Matthew 5:8)

A Child in Rio De Janeiro

Child psychiatrist Robert Coles stood on a hill in Rio De Janeiro; with him was a ten year old from the slums. Looking out at sea, the child said softly, "If I had a choice to pick the way I'd die, I'd choose to be carried off by the wind over the ocean. I'd be made clean twice before I saw his face."[1]

The boy, who had seen more physical and moral filth than most children his age, expressed a common human hope–and fear. He hoped that when he died he would see God. But he feared that in his present state he was not pure enough for that face-to-face meeting.

That boy's hope is echoed in 1 Corinthians 13:12 where the Apostle Paul says of our better future: "For now we see in a mirror, dimly, but then we will see face to face." You will recall from the previous session that Jacob expressed his joy at the peaceful meeting with Esau by saying, "For truly to see your face is like seeing the face of God." (Genesis 33:10)

The Young Isaiah

As old as our belief in God, as deep as our desire to be in God's presence, is also the fear that we are not pure enough to see God's face. **Isaiah 6:1-8** tells of the terror of the young prophet when he had a vision of the Lord. Read that passage now. Note how Isaiah dates his vision at the end of Uzziah's reign. At that time, in the temple in Jerusalem, he saw God sitting on a heavenly throne, surrounded by heavenly attendants. In desperation he cried out:

---

1   Robert Coles, *The Moral Life of Children* (Boston/New York: The Atlantic Monthly Press, 1986), p. 1.

> Woe is me! I am lost, for I am a man of unclean lips, and I live among a people
> of unclean lips; yet my eyes have seen the King, the Lord of hosts! (6:5)

According to biblical tradition, no human could look on God's face and live. The fear of God's presence goes back to one of the earliest stories in Genesis, when Eve and Adam ate the forbidden fruit.

> Then the eyes of both were opened, and they knew that they were naked; and they sewed fig leaves together and made loincloths for themselves. Then they heard the sound of the Lord God walking in the garden at the time of the evening breeze, and the man and his wife hid themselves from the presence of the Lord God among the trees of the garden. (Genesis 3:7-8)

Moses begged to see God's glory. But he was told, "You cannot see my face, for no one shall see me and live." (Exodus 33:20) No wonder Isaiah was terror-stricken when he "saw the Lord sitting on a throne." (Isaiah 6:1) Yet Isaiah did not die. He was saved when one of the heavenly attendants touched his mouth with a hot coal taken from the altar. The altar was the appointed place where sacrifices for sin were made. By being touched with fire from the place of sacrifice, Isaiah was purified. Though he had seen God, he was allowed to live.

The Transfiguration

The account of Isaiah's temple vision helps us with one of the most mystifying stories about Jesus. It is known as the Transfiguration. It is told in **Matthew 17:1-8**. Read that text now.

Jesus takes the inner circle of disciples, Peter and James and John, to a hilltop. There he is suddenly touched with the divine glory, with that which makes God utterly different from God's creatures. Jesus' clothing becomes a dazzling white; his face is radiant. And the disciples see the great Hebrew prophets, Moses and Elijah, talking with him. Even Isaiah's vision didn't include Moses and Elijah!

Peter, with more courage than good sense, suggests that they build three tents, one for each of these glorious personages. But suddenly from a bright cloud come these words, "This is my Son, the Beloved; with him I am well pleased; listen to him." (17:5) Now properly terrified, the disciples fall to the ground and hide their faces. They do not want to look at divinity; they know what happens to those who behold the glory of the Lord. But Jesus reassures them, and when they look up, Jesus is alone and the glory has departed.

Is It Prattle?

In the study group in which I tested this material, we were solemnly discussing Isaiah's vision and the Transfiguration. What might it mean, we wondered, to see God? A retired clergyman in the group, who had kept silent, burst out in indignation: "This is all a lot of prattle!" He touched his eyes with his fingers. "These eyes can't see God." And then he quoted to us from the First Letter of John: "No one has ever seen God; if we love one another, God lives in us, and his love is perfected in us." (1 John 4:12)

We asked him about mystics such as Theresa of Avila and St. John of the Cross, who had so purified their lives and thoughts that they had come into God's presence. He said he knew about "beatific visions," but for himself, he did not expect to have them.

Drawing on the clergyman's quotation from 1 John and the account of the Transfiguration, I tried to state what I understood to be his position: "Do you mean that we are tempted to be like Peter? We would rather be up on the mountain having unusual spiritual experiences than follow Jesus back down into the valley where people need our love and help?" He nodded his agreement.

Purity of Heart

Our study group moved away from talking about visions of God to ask what Jesus might have meant by the first part of the Beatitude, "Blessed are the pure in heart." We confessed to our imperfections. As one member of the group wryly observed, "Well, even Mother Teresa has bad days." That led to a consideration of our need for God's forgiveness. And when the session ended, we were talking about the Lord's Supper.

That seems right. For the sacrament of the Lord's Supper–together with Baptism–links "purity of heart" to "seeing God." In a beloved Communion hymn we sing:

> Here, O my Lord, I see Thee face to face;
> Here would I touch and handle things unseen ..."

> Here would I lay aside each earthly load,
> Here taste afresh the calm of sin forgiven.[2]

---

2   "Here, O My Lord, I See Thee Face To Face."

One writer says of the Rev. Hortius Bonar, author of that hymn: "Purity of soul, holiness of life, personal abandon to Christ were part and parcel of the man."[3]

The sacraments are visible signs of the invisible actions of God. The Spirit of God is present to cleanse those being baptized, making them fit to be gathered into the company of God's holy people. In the Supper, the Spirit confirms the new covenant God has made with us through Jesus Christ. The Supper is also a promise that one day, like the first disciples, we shall sit face-to-face with our risen Lord at table in God's Kingdom.

The Puritans

In a discussion of purity of heart, one group that readily comes to mind is the Puritans. Many people in North America are both the spiritual and the physical descendants of these British Christians. Like the clergyman I mentioned above, the Puritans were impatient with mere talk about the glories of heaven. Nor did they passively rely on the sacraments to make them clean within. They set out to purify the church, themselves, and their society. And when they got discouraged with cleaning up England, they went to New England. As one boatload of them left for Massachusetts in 1630, John Winthrop said to them, "We shall be as a city upon a hill. We must love brotherly without dissimulations; we must love each other with a pure heart fervently."[4]

How does one acquire a pure heart? Surely one of the most revealing Puritan texts is John Bunyan's *Pilgrim's Progress*. It is an extended allegory of the Christian life, in which "Christian" makes his difficult way to the Celestial City. (This is similar to the metaphor of the Way of Discipleship offered in the Introduction to this series.)

One of Christian's stops is the House of the Interpreter. While he is in a very dusty parlor, a man comes in to sweep. Such a cloud of dust is raised that Christian is almost choked to death. Then Interpreter asks a girl to sprinkle the room with water. When this is done, the sweeping continues until the room is clean. When Christian asks the meaning of this, the Interpreter explains:

> This parlor is the heart of a man that was never sanctified by the sweet grace of the gospel. The dust is his original sin, and inward corruptions, that have defiled the whole man. He that began to sweep at first is the law; but she that brought water, and did sprinkle it, is the Gospel … the law, instead of cleansing the heart … from sin, doth … increase it in the soul … As thou sawest the damsel lay

---

3 William Chalmers Covert and Calvin Weiss Laufer eds., *Handbook to the Hymnal* (Philadelphia: Presbyterian Board of Christian Education, 1935), p. 373.

4 Strauss and Howe, *Generations*, p. 121.

the dust by sprinkling the floor with water, so is sin vanquished and subdued, and the soul made clean, through the faith of it, and consequently made fit for the King of glory to inhabit.[5]

But, purity of heart is not a simple matter. Some of us received a Puritan upbringing, in which cleanliness was thought to be a sign of godliness. When we used bad language, we had our mouths washed out with soap. We were taught that alcohol and tobacco would defile our bodies. Certain books were judged not fit for us to read. We were taught very little about sex, either at home or in church; there was the lurking notion that somehow it was impure.

Now we have been taught by our society to look back in amusement on such practices. We refer to the Puritan work ethic with something akin to pity. And we use the adjective puritanical more to condemn than to praise. We do not want to be called "Puritans" any more than we want to be called "Pharisees."

Perhaps the connection between these two groups is worth noting here. The Pharisees of Jesus' day were not unlike the Puritans of the seventeenth century. They were very zealous for the religious life. Jesus, you may remember, got into deep trouble with them. They saw him being friends with publicans and sinners and accused him of consorting with the unclean. Jesus, for his part, accused them of washing the outside of the cup but leaving the inside dirty. It is possible that "Blessed are the pure in heart" was spoken with the Pharisees in mind.

A Sign along the Way

As one of the signs along the Way of Discipleship, what does the Fourth Beatitude say to us today? Surely it warns us that purity is not something to be taken lightly. If we are anxious about our self-worth, fearful that like Isaiah, "I am a man of unclean lips, and I live among a people of unclean lips," that is nothing to be shrugged off. If the central rituals of the church are signs of cleansing, then purity – holiness – must be a major concern of us all.

It need not be a crippling concern. We can take a lesson from the experiences of Isaiah and the disciples on the Mount of Transfiguration. We can learn from the excesses of the Puritans. Isaiah was purified so that he might be fit to become God's spokesperson. The disciples were granted the vision on the Mount of Transfiguration so that they might be equipped for missionary work back down in the valley. The Puritans settled in North America to build a New Jerusalem.

---

5 John Bunyan, *The Pilgrim's Progress from This World to That Which Is to Come* (New York: Hurst and Co.), pp. 96-97.

How can we be pure without becoming puritanical? How can congregations be holy without becoming "holier than thou"? Those are the difficult questions to which this Beatitude asks us to respond.

FOR FURTHER STUDY AND REFLECTION

Memory Bank

> Isaiah 6:1-8
>
> Matthew 5:8

Research

1. Psalm 24 makes a connection between "clean hands and pure hearts" (verse 4) and "the company of those who seek the face of Jacob" (verse 6). Check a commentary on Psalms to see how this connection is described.

2. Select one of the mystical writings of Theresa of Avila, St. John of the Cross, Brother Lawrence, Soren Kierkegaard, or Thomas Kelly and review what they have to say about purity of heart and seeing God.

3. Review what Jesus says in the rest of the Sermon on the Mount (Matthew 5:13-7:29) about inward righteousness.

Reflection

1. In his poem, "I Live Yet Do Not Live in Me," St. John of the Cross confesses:

> When I begin to feel relief
>
> on seeing you in the sacrament,
>
> I sink in deeper discontent,
>
> deprived of your sweet company.
>
> Now everything compels my grief:
>
> I want – yet can't – see you nearby,
>
> and die because I do not die.[6]

---

6   *The Poems of Saint John of the Cross* (New York: New Directions Publishing Corp., 1972), p. 65.

In what way do his words reflect the challenge of seeking holiness in the midst of life?

2. Read Jesus' Parable of the Pharisee and the Tax Collector in Luke 18:9-14. How can we seek purity of heart and life without falling into the trap of self-righteousness?

Blessed Are You

SUMMARY

Peacemaking, which is especially pleasing to God, requires us to be both innocent of malice and wise to the ways of the world. Jesus demonstrated both capacities.

BASIC BIBLE REFERENCES

The Book of Esther
Matthew 5:9; 21:1-11

WORD LIST

fulfillment
grand vizier
Holocaust
Joab
Messiah
millennium
Nebuchadnezzar
Passover
pogrom
Purim
redeemer
shalom
Xerxes (Ahasuerus)

5

THE PEACEMAKERS

Blessed are the peacemakers,
for they will be called children of God.
(MATTHEW 5:9)

A Massacre in Hebron

On February 25th, 1994, a Jewish settler entered a mosque in the town of Hebron in the Occupied Territories. Armed with an automatic rifle, he opened fire and killed twenty-nine Muslim worshippers. Reactions to the massacre were mixed. Some condemned him as a terrorist. A woman, writing to our local newspaper, said he acted only to prevent a massacre of Jews. The killings had the immediate effect of delaying the process by which Israelis and Palestinians sought to achieve a permanent peace.

To some observers it seemed ironic that the Hebron massacre took place during the Feast of Purim. These are the days in which Jews remember their deliverance from ethnic cleansing in the time of Esther. One poet asked:

> What has happened to reason
> since someone deconstructed the text
> of Esther with an automatic weapon
> that made Joab look like a canonized saint
> in contrast to Dr. Goldstein from Brooklyn?[1]

The Story of Esther

The Book of Esther provides a vivid backdrop for the consideration of why Jesus singled out peacemakers for a special blessing. The story is set in the reign of Xerxes I, whose Persian Empire stretched from Ethiopia to India. He ruled during the period 485 – 464 B.C.

---

1   Kemmer Anderson, "Hebron 1994," *The Christian Century*, 6 April 1994, p. 356.

In the Bible his name is given as Ahasuerus. Living in his capital city of Susa were Jews whose ancestors had been carried into exile by Nebuchadnezzar a century before.

Read quickly through the **Book of Esther** to get the story line. The introductory material in a study Bible will also be helpful. As you will see, the story opens with an account of Ahasuerus's displeasure with his queen and his determination to replace her. A call goes out for beautiful virgins. One of those who responds is a Jew named Mordecai. He puts forward his cousin, Esther, who is also his adopted daughter. She joins the royal harem. In due time Esther finds favor with the emperor and is crowned his queen.

Meanwhile, Mordecai has earned the wrath of Haman, Ahasuerus's vizier. Haman schemes to destroy all the Jews living in the kingdom. Esther discovers the plotted pogrom and schemes to foil Haman and save her people. So successful is she in interceding with the emperor, that not only are the Jews saved, but they are allowed to take revenge on their enemies. Haman, along with his sons, is hanged; thousands of others are killed. Esther and Mordecai send out a letter to all Jews in the kingdom, "wishing peace and security to all" (9:30) and fixing certain days as *Purim*, a feast to commemorate the Jews' deliverance.

Just a Fairy Tale?

Sounds like something out of the Arabian Nights, doesn't it? A beautiful queen, a wicked vizier, a foiled plot, a rescued people. Some critics call it a fairy tale. However, when you read the Book of Esther, you get the messy details: intrigue, lies, murder, revenge, oppression, slaughter, ethnic cleansing. Sounds less like a fairy tale than it does like what we read in our daily newspapers. Have things changed much in twenty-four centuries? The same things that cause wars in our time were operating in the time of Esther: imperial ambition, political intrigue, ethnic hatred, oppressed minorities, massacres of the innocents.

Some members of your study group may object to the use of the Book of Esther in a discussion of peacemaking. For them the narrative is too violent, too bloody, too full of cruelty and revenge. But the story, if nothing else, helps us keep our feet on the blood-soaked ground that is our earth. If we keep the story of Esther in the back of our minds as we discuss peacemaking, we are not likely to deal lightly with human conflict.

The Book of Esther also serves this purpose: It reminds us of the precarious existence of the people of Israel during the millennium preceding Jesus' birth. It provides a political framework for the hope and expectation of the advent of the Messiah. Judah and Israel were tiny states surrounded by large and rapacious nations. Jesus, like Esther, appeared when a brutal empire had the Jews by the throat.

While Esther may not fit everyone's image of a peacemaker, she *did* save her people from ethnic cleansing. She risked her life to prevent a great injustice. She was a rescuer. As such, she was a prototype, a shadow of the Redeemer who was to come. It was people like Esther that gave Israel hope for a Messiah, for One who would put down all enemies and establish God's people in peace.

A Different Peacemaker

Jesus was believed by many of his contemporaries to be that Messiah. His extraordinary actions and words created in hearts the hope that he was the longed-for Redeemer. No wonder there was a huge popular demonstration when Jesus came to Jerusalem for the Feast of Passover. Passover celebrated the deliverance of Israel from the tyranny of Egypt. Jerusalem was the city of Ruth's grandson, David, Israel's great tenth-century king. During David's reign the people had enjoyed peace and security. The name Jerusalem had within it the Hebrew word for peace, *shalom*.

When he entered the City of David, Jesus did an extraordinary thing. You will find the details in **Matthew 21:1-11**. Read that passage now. Instead of riding into Jerusalem on a horse, as befits a valiant warrior, Jesus rode in on a donkey. Whatever a donkey symbolizes, it is not martial supremacy and political power!

The author of Matthew's Gospel saw this act as the fulfillment of an oracle from the prophet Zechariah:

> Rejoice greatly, O daughter Zion!
>   Shout aloud, O daughter Jerusalem.
> Lo, your king comes to you;
>   triumphant and victorious is he,
>   humble and riding on a donkey,
>   on a colt, the foal of a donkey.
>
> He will cut off the chariot from Ephraim
>   and the war horse from Jerusalem;
> and the battle bow shall be cut off,
>   and he shall command peace to the nations.   (Zechariah 9:9-10.)

As Jesus rode into the city, an enthusiastic crowd went before and behind, shouting: "Hosanna to the Son of David." (Matthew 21:9) And when he entered the city, all Jerusalem was in turmoil. Who was he? Was he truly the Messiah? No one knew for sure. "The crowds were saying, 'This is the prophet Jesus from Nazareth in Galilee'." (Matthew 21:11)

By entering Jerusalem on a donkey, Jesus made a radical statement about the Messiah as peacemaker. Contrary to many hopes, he would not be a victorious general–not a Jewish Julius Caesar. Such hopes were futile. The might of oppressive empires would not be overthrown by force of arms.

If you want Jesus' own commentary on his entry into Jerusalem, look at what he told the disciples about their mission: "See, I am sending you out like sheep in the midst of wolves; so be wise as serpents and innocent as doves." (Matthew 10:16) By riding into Jerusalem on a donkey, Jesus demonstrated both wisdom and innocence. The dovish serpent was set as the model for the Christian peacemaker.

Serpents and Doves

We have not pictured peacemakers in that way, have we? Christians have tended to play off against each other two very different models of the peacemaker: the hawk and the dove. People like Esther, who used power and weaponry to secure justice and freedom, are classified as hawks. The nonviolent, who refuse the levers of power and the instruments of death, are classified as doves. And here, some would say, we have the choice set before Christians who would make peace.

Some argue that Esther, for all her courage, represents a failed strategy. Intrigue, power politics, ethnic strife, vengeance – these will never deliver peace. The use of force serves only to keep the cycle of war and vengeance spinning.

But others claim that the renunciation of armed struggle is not good enough. If hawks cannot win the peace, neither can doves. One must be open-eyed about the world we live in. If wars are to be avoided, or at least kept within just limits, diplomacy, armaments, and the threat of retaliation are necessary.

Do we have to choose to be either hawks or doves? What if we take as our model the reputed Messiah who entered Jerusalem on a donkey? What if we interpret that as an enactment of what it means to be "wise as serpents and as innocent as doves?"

Peacemakers will always be sheep in the midst of wolves, with never strong enough teeth or sharp enough claws to prevail. Therefore they must be innocent of malice; they must renounce revenge and retaliation. But they must also be wise to the ways of the world; they must not suppose that simply refusing to fight is a winning strategy for achieving peace.

Such an interpretation shifts the emphasis from politically correct *thinking* about peace to a strategy for *making peace*. It was those who are peacemakers whom Jesus blessed; these he said would be called "children of God." Using our energies to debate the merits of hawks vs. doves is to wander from the Way of Discipleship. It is a trip down a side road into a dead end.

In Your Congregation

Let's shift the scene to your congregation, where you probably have both hawks and doves. Doves are the folk who will have peace at any price; they will do anything to avoid quarrels; they think that conflict within a church is tragic. And then there are the hawks. They do not shrink from the use of power, even intrigue, if that seems called for. They seem to thrive on conflict; some treat human relations as a kind of body-contact sport. Each type thinks of the other with pity or contempt. Doves think the hawks care only for themselves, not for the peace of the church. The hawks secretly think of the doves as wimps or hopelessly idealistic or blind to the realities of a world where the wolves feed on the sheep.

But isn't the division of members into hawks and doves in itself a cause of conflict? Jesus did not divide the world, or the church, into these categories. Rather he saw Christians as sheep in the midst of wolves. Therefore he advised his disciples to be wise as serpents and innocent as doves. Being a peacemaker is a great deal more difficult and costly than choosing to fight or not to fight!

One day while I was eating lunch in a restaurant in San Bernardino, California, I saw a young man sitting in a booth with this inscription on the back of his shirt: "Peacemakers who sow peace, raise a harvest of righteousness." He has it right: Peacemakers are those who act for peace – who sow peace, work for peace, pray for peace, make peace.

Who Are the Peacemakers?

Who are outstanding peacemakers in our generation? Since World War II the Nobel Peace Prize has been given to people from a variety of nations and vocations. Among them are Mairead Corrigan-Maguire (Northern Ireland), Mother Teresa (Albania), Mikhail Gorbachev (U.S.S.R.), Desmond Tutu, Nelson Mandela, F.W. de Klerk (South Africa), Henry Kissinger and Martin Luther King, Jr. (U.S.A.), and Daw Aung San Suu Kyi (Burma).

As I was preparing this discussion of "Blessed are the peacemakers," I found these references in the newspapers of my home town of Santa Fe. A letter to the editor of *The New Mexican* said:

> We need a strong mayor who will work for social justice and help us heal. We need a leader who will respect the diverse values of our community, who doesn't confuse anger with strength, and who is not beholden to special-interest groups. Linda Durham stands out among the mayoral candidates as a strong and gentle peacemaker.[2]

Then there was an Associated Press account of the women who are codirectors of a group that tries to get pro-choice and anti-abortion folks to engage in dialogue. The article referred to Mary Jacksteit, a Presbyterian laywoman, and Sister Adrienne Kaufmann, a Benedictine nun, as "the peacemakers."[3]

My nomination would be those "righteous Gentiles" who rescued Jews from death at the hands of the Third Reich. In some respects they are like Esther, saving people from a dreadful pogrom. In other ways they fit the model suggested by Jesus: rather than taking up arms in futile resistance against overwhelming force, they were "wise as serpents and innocent as doves" in saving those they could.

Consider the Czech manufacturer featured in the film *Schindler's List*. One of the Jews who was rescued by him said in an interview:

> Out of 80 million Germans, you find one premiere individual who stood up against a mighty power and decided to do something to the machinery that could have ground him down. He took it upon himself to do this. I believe if only a thousand Germans had stood up and done the same thing, the entire population of Jews could have been saved. But there was only one Oskar Schindler. And he did this so beautifully, never demanding anything in return ... Schindler was a savior of humanity. He assured us that there are people who will come forward and help others in need.[4]

---

2   *The New Mexican*, 26 February 1994, p. A-7.

3   *The New Mexican*, 19 February 1994, p. B-5.

4   Interview with Leopold Pfefferberg, *Santa Fe Sun*, April 1994, p. 8.

There were others. There was the Polish couple, Alex and Mela Roslan, who took into their home an eight-year-old Jewish child, saving him from the Holocaust. When interviewed some forty years later, Alex said:

> The best years of my life were when I first came to Warsaw and became successful in business. And then I was so happy when I brought Jacob home. No one was paying me, but I felt I was doing something great. I thought, *if I survive this, I've done something great.*[5]

Whom would you nominate as peacemakers in your generation? As those deserving to be called "children of God"?

FOR FURTHER STUDY AND REFLECTION

Memory Bank

Esther 9:26-27
Matthew 5:9; 21:9

Research

1. Ask a Jewish friend to describe the festival of Purim or read an article about it in an encyclopedia of religion.

2. The Greek translation of the Old Testament (the Septuagint) contains several additions to the Book of Esther. If you have a study Bible, they will probably be in the section containing the Apocrypha. Review the additions and note how they differ from the book in the Hebrew canon.

3. *The Interpreter's Dictionary of the Bible* lists these scriptural warrants for the observance of the Feast of Passover: Exodus 12:1-13:16; 23:15; 34:18-20, 25; Leviticus 23:4-14; Numbers 28:16-25; Deuteronomy 16:1-8. Look up several of these texts and compare them with the mandate for the Festival of Purim in Esther 9:24-32.

4. If you have a friend or acquaintance who belongs to one of the traditional "Peace churches" (Mennonites, Brethren, Friends) ask him or her to describe the church's position on peacemaking.

---

5 Gay Block and Malka Drucker, *Rescuers: Portraits of Moral Courage in the Holocaust* (New York: Holmes and Meier Inc., 1992), p, 191.

Reflection

1. Gay Block, who did interviews and photos for the book on the Gentile Rescuers, says there were four roles for persons in the days of the Holocaust: the victims, the oppressors, the rescuers, and the bystanders. She says those roles have not changed with respect to conflicts today. To what extent do you agree with her? Where are the peacemakers in that picture?

2. A member of our congregation wrote the following comment about peacemaking:

   Jesus' refusal to use violence or to resist arrest led to his crucifixion. Mahatma Gandhi and Martin Luther King, Jr., are two twentieth-century leaders who were also committed to nonviolence, and who also were killed by their enemies. Is Jesus' teaching too idealistic to be followed in the kind of world we live in? Think of the conflicts between Jews and Arabs, Protestants and Catholics in Northern Ireland, the ethnic struggles in Central Europe.

   How would you respond to his question?

BLESSED ARE YOU

SUMMARY

Those who follow Jesus may expect, like him, to encounter rejection and worse. Social justice requires sacrifice. But such sacrifice bestows happiness.

BASIC BIBLE REFERENCES

Amos 7:10-17
Matthew 5:6, 10-12; 16:13-28

WORD LIST

Amaziah
Israel
Judah
oracle
prophet
righteousness
social justice

6

THE PROPHETS OF RIGHTEOUSNESS

*Blessed are those who hunger and thirst for righteousness,
for they will be filled.*
(MATTHEW 5:6)
*Blessed are those who are persecuted for righteousness' sake,
for theirs is the kingdom of heaven.*
(MATTHEW 5:10)
*Blessed are you when people revile you and utter all kinds of
evil against you falsely on my account. Rejoice and be glad,
for your reward is great in heaven, for in the same way they
persecuted the prophets who were before you.*
(MATTHEW 5:11-12)

Prophets of Righteousness

In 1976 Aleksandr Solzhenitsyn, the Russian novelist and historian whom we mentioned in Chapter One, moved to Vermont. He had been expelled from the Soviet Union for his criticism of the Establishment. Although he was recognized world-wide as a symbol of anti-Communism, Solzhenitsyn was not invited to the White House. The president's advisors thought the visit might be an embarrassment. And no wonder. Listen to what Solzhenitsyn said about the West in one of his speeches:

> Freedom! To fill people's mailboxes, eyes, ears, and brains with commercial rubbish against their will, television programs that are impossible to watch with a sense of coherence … Freedom! For publishers and film producers to poison the younger generations with corrupting filth. Freedom! For adolescents of fourteen to eighteen to immerse themselves in idleness and pleasure instead of intensive study and spiritual growth.[1]

In the eighth century before Christ, an ex-herdsman named Amos arrived in Israel from the southern country of Judah. In public speeches he began to scold the Establishment. Surely

---

1 Aleksandr Solzhenitsyn, quoted in David Remnick, "Profile: The Exile Returns," *The New Yorker*, 14 February 1994, p. 70.

to the ears of the good citizens of Israel his words were no more welcome than Solzhenitsyn's are to ours. Here is a sample of Amos's preaching:

> Hear this word, you cows of Bashan who are on Mount Samaria,
>   who oppress the poor, who crush the needy,
>   who say to their husbands, "Bring something to drink!"

> The Lord God has sworn by his holiness:
>   The time is surely coming upon you,
>   when they shall take you away with hooks,
>   even the last of you with fishhooks.   (Amos 4:1-2)

In the time between Amos and our era, there appeared in Galilee of Judea a young preacher of righteousness. Jesus went to the capital city of Jerusalem and pronounced these woes on the Establishment:

> Woe to you, scribes and Pharisees, hypocrites! For you build the tombs of the prophets and decorate the graves of the righteous, and you say, "If we had lived in the days of our ancestors, we would not have taken part with them in shedding the blood of the prophets" … You snakes, you brood of vipers! How can you escape being sentenced to hell?   (Matthew 23:29-33)

Amos of Tekoa

Jesus blessed those who "hunger and thirst for righteousness," those who are "persecuted for righteousness' sake," those who suffer "falsely on my account." And these he links to the Hebrew prophets, who preached God's righteousness and were persecuted and sometimes killed.

If there is one person in all of Scripture who deserves the title "preacher of righteousness," it is Amos of Tekoa. His oracles are preserved in the biblical book that bears his name. He is numbered among the prophets although he never claimed that title. He was not a professional who earned his living by oracular pronouncements. He was a shepherd and arborist, and he would have preferred to remain in Judah, following his flocks and caring for his trees. But he was driven to leave his country, to go north to Israel. At the heart of that kingdom, in the king's own sanctuary, Amos pronounced Israel's doom. For her lack of social righteousness, he said, her king would be killed and she would go into exile.

This was a harsh message. Skim chapters 3-6 for Amos' indictment of Israel. His vision of the coming devastation is found in Chapters 7-9. In **Amos 7:10-17** we hear what happened as a consequence of his preaching. Read that passage now. Amos was confronted by the chief priest, Amaziah, and told to go back home and leave Israel alone. He was treated as we would likely treat someone who came from a neighboring country and read us a list of our sins. The bumper sticker, *America: Love It or Leave It*, says it all.

At Caesarea Philippi

Fast-forward about seven hundred years to the northern reaches of Judea, not far from where Amos had been branded a troublemaker. Another preacher is stirring up the populace and making the Establishment down in Jerusalem very nervous. His name is Jesus of Nazareth. Read **Matthew 16:13-28**, which tells about a critical moment in his career. He is planning to take his mission to the capital city. First he wants to take some soundings of public opinion. "What are the folks saying about me?" he asks his followers.

The most widespread opinion is that he is a prophet in the line of Elijah and Isaiah and Amos. But one of his followers is given an illuminating flash. Peter says, "You are the Messiah, the Son of the Living God." (16:16) Jesus is not only a preacher of righteousness, he is the bringer of righteousness, the one who will usher in the age of justice and peace!

Jesus then tells the disciples what is going to happen. He will go to Jerusalem, he will confront the Establishment, and they will kill him. Peter takes him off to one side and remonstrates: "God forbid it, Lord! This must never happen to you." (16:22) Like Amaziah confronted by Amos, Peter reacts in a very human, common sense way. It was unthinkable to Amaziah that God's Chosen People would be smashed and scattered. It is unthinkable to Peter that the Messiah should suffer death.

Jesus turns on Peter and says, "Get behind me, Satan! You are a stumbling block to me; for you are setting your mind not on divine things but on human things." (16:23) Then Jesus tells the disciples that if they follow him, they may expect no better treatment at the hands of the Establishment. They, like him, must "take up their crosses." They will be persecuted for righteousness sake, as the prophets were before them.

A Reversal

Peter and the others had to come to terms with a reversal of their expectations of the Messiah. They hoped for a victorious prince; they were given a crucified prophet. But are not many of the Beatitudes reversals of human expectations? We hope for financial security and hear from Jesus: "Blessed are the poor in spirit." We long for the relief of grief and an end to weeping. We hear: "Blessed are those who mourn." Our counselors and sages tell us to assert our best selves. Jesus says: "Blessed are the meek." And now, still haunted by stories of slavery and oppression and the Holocaust, we hear from the Redeemer: "Blessed are those who are persecuted." "Blessed are you when people revile you and persecute you and utter all kinds of evil against you falsely on my account."

Those who are called to follow Jesus cannot think first of bread and home and pleasant meadows and all the familiar and comforting things. In a reversal of all human hopes and expectations, they are to think first of righteousness, of God's purposes and not their own. And in return they are promised happiness. In the Lord's Prayer, do we not first pray for the coming of God's righteous rule and only then ask for bread? If we put God's cause ahead of our own, we may expect God to take care of all our needs.

Your Preacher

Not only in our prayers, but in our preaching and hearing of God's Word this reversal of expectations needs to be acknowledged. When your preacher stands in the pulpit on Sunday morning, he or she may take the text for the sermon from the Book of Amos. One of the favorite texts for Dr. Martin Luther King, Jr., was Amos 5:21-24:

> I hate, I despise your festivals,
>> and I take no delight in your solemn assemblies …

> Take away from me the noise of your songs;
>> I will not listen to the melody of your harps.

> But let justice roll down like waters,
>> and righteousness like an everflowing stream.

What is the response of your congregation to the proclamation of social justice? To the condemnation of religion that is empty of righteousness? What will you do? Will you identify with the message, however painful, however critical of your community and your society? Or will you say to your preacher, as Amaziah did to Amos, "Go back home; your calling is to be a shepherd, a pastor, not a troublemaker." Will you make the preacher or the prophet the scapegoat for the sins of society and run him or her out of town?

The fact that your preacher voices strong criticism of our society ought not to be, by itself, reason for unhappiness. There may be blessing for the entire congregation if it chooses to stand with a preacher of righteousness against the established order. Jesus promised, did he not, that there was blessing to be found in persecution for righteousness' sake?

My role as a columnist for a denominational magazine once plunged me into a lively correspondence with a layman in Columbus, Ohio. We debated the meaning of "promoting social righteousness," one of the stated goals of our denomination. My correspondent wanted to limit that goal to declaring to others the righteousness we have in Christ through faith. He did not want his church embarked on a crusade for social justice. He wrote:

> Promoting social righteousness means spreading throughout society the good
> news of salvation through Jesus Christ ... Christians are New Testament people,
> Jesus people ... the word "justice" doesn't appear anywhere in the KJV, RSV,
> or NRSV of the New Testament.

Probably that layman speaks for a good many folks in the pews of our churches. They do not want the injustices of society condemned from the pulpit, not in public statements of the denomination, nor in denominational literature. They argue that such preachments only stir up trouble and make church members unhappy and dissatisfied.

But surely happiness in congregational life is more than an absence of conflict over social issues. Remember the image of the Christian life that underlies this series: a group of people are climbing a high and narrow way that leads to the City of God. True, Christians do not build that city with blueprints and plans and organized schemes. Neither is it attained without conflict, without sacrifice, without suffering. And in some paradoxical way, which makes very little psychological sense, there is joy in that struggle and peace in the midst of that conflict.

The Balcony and the Road

One of my heroes in theological seminary was John Mackay, a missionary statesman of the highest order. Mackay's favorite metaphor was the Balcony and the Road. Christians belong on the road, not on the balcony, he was fond of telling audiences. To be engaged, involved, down in the streets where the action is, that is where one is present with Christ. Mackay despised the detachment, the leisure, the hypocrisy of those who were only spectators of life's struggles.

I was reminded of John Mackay's metaphor recently. My wife and I made our first visit to New Orleans to attend a reunion. Our hotel was on Bourbon Street, and the hospitality suite for our group was on the second floor, with a balcony that overlooked the street. One Saturday night we stood at the railing of the balcony and watched the folks parading back and forth below. How much freer, how much happier, how much more glad the revelers in the street seemed than we watchers on the balcony.

Do you recall from the discussion of the fifth Beatitude the comments of Gay Block, who interviewed the Righteous Gentiles? In times of social conflict, she said, there are only four roles: the oppressor, the victim, the bystander, and the rescuer. It is not the bystander, the onlooker, the viewer whom God will bless. It is the one who follows in the footsteps of the Redeemer. Are we not likely to find our greatest joy in following Christ on the Way to the New Jerusalem, no matter what the cost?

FOR FURTHER STUDY AND REFLECTION

Memory Bank

> Amos 5:24
> Matthew 5:6, 10-12

Research

1. Examine Jesus' teaching about God's righteous rule in the Parables of the Kingdom in Matthew 13:24-30, 36-43; 20:1-16; 21:28-32; 25:31-46. How does this teaching relate to your understanding of Matthew 5:6, 10-12?

2. Review the meanings given for "righteousness" and "justice" in a Bible dictionary or theological word book. Compare that information with what you gleaned in the activity above.

Reflection

1. To what extent do you agree with the following comments on the prophets and Jesus?

   It is true that these 8th century prophets, Amos, Hosea, Isaiah, and Micah, were ethical prophets, for they insisted with the utmost firmness and resolution upon right action and fair dealing between man and man ... Nevertheless, to say that they were ethical prophets and no more is to say less than the truth, because they showed a marked bias in favor of the poor and needy, and this bias is indissolubly bound up with their notions of righteousness.[2]

   Jesus is on the side of the marginalized, the immigrants, the victims of prejudice, no doubt about it. But his attitude is far from that of democratic good will;

---

2 Alan Richardson, ed., *A Theological Word Book of the Bible* (New York: The Macmillan Company, 1950), p. 202.

he's no bleeding heart ... The wealthy, whom he invites to give their goods away, are against him, but so are the unions, middle-class peasants and workers. In each case he goes only part of the way with them. But anyone is welcome to receive his message, though he gives special mention to those whom history grinds into oblivion, the raw material with which nations fight their wars, their leaders constantly talking about the happiness of future generations while accepting the present sacrifices of the wretched of the earth.[3]

2. Many of the Beatitudes involve reversals of our expectations. Review Matthew 5:3-12 and select one or two Beatitudes that offer the greatest challenge to you. In what ways do these sayings challenge the way you look at life?

---

3   Jean Sulivan, *Morning Light* (New York: Paulist Press, 1976), p. 50.

NOTES

NOTES

NOTES